B.A.S.I.C. TRAINING

BECOMING ARMED SOLDIERS IN CHRIST

B.A.S.I.C. TRAINING

BECOMING ARMED SOLDIERS IN CHRIST

Schledia Anderson

THREE KEYS PUBLISHING

UNLOCKING WORLDS, HEARTS, AND MINDS

ISBN softcover: 978-0-9887597-5-6

Published in the United States

THREE KEYS PUBLISHING
www.threekeyspublishing.com

DEDICATION

To the soldiers in God's Army who have gone on before us, having fought the good fight and paving the way.

ACKNOWLEDGMENTS

First and foremost, I want to thank God for saving me from the bottom of the miry clay and setting my feet on the Rock, a sure foundation. I cannot go without thanking Milt and Joyce Green who have gone on to be with the Lord. Their teachings have given me the meat of the Word and helped to bring me to the place I am today. A special thank you to my friend Laurie Corson who encouraged me years ago to put the teachings the Lord had given me into book format to allow others to glean from them. William Hancock, thank you for your input and review. I would like to thank my husband, Colby Anderson, for encouraging me and having faith in me as a woman of God.

CONTENTS

Introduction

This book comes from a teaching the Lord gave me in 2004 for a youth group I was pastoring at the time. While it was originally given to me to teach teenagers, it contains truths needed by the entire body. It is broken down into sections and parts for easy weekly use in Sunday school classes, study groups, or youth groups. Taught on a weekly basis, the course will last seven weeks. There are object lessons and games in the back that can be used to demonstrate the lessons. One thing I've learned is that we all grasp concepts and teachings better when we are given a visual. Each person in the group should have his or her own book so they can prepare for the lesson beforehand and be ready for discussion. Each lesson ends with a group of questions for reflection.

INTRODUCTION

"Sand Castles"

Sand castles are made by little boys and girls,
Creating for themselves imaginary worlds.
They start out with a bucket and a shovel or two,
They dig up the sand and add water for glue.
Placing patty upon patty, they stretch their tower to the sky,
Carving out windows way up high.
Once the tower is erected and tall,
That is when they start on the wall.
As they mold it and shape it, securing it in place,
They add to the wall—one large gate.
A moat is then dug all the way around,
To keep out the beasts that cannot be bound.
The sand castle is protected by a moat and a wall;
Unfortunately, a world made of sand will eventually fall.

The poem "Sand Castles" is taken from my Young Adult novel, *Plain Jane*. I felt it fit perfectly with the mission of my foundational teaching ministry. When a world is built of sand, it will eventually collapse, just as when a life is built upon sand, it will not withstand the wind and the waves.

Luke 6:46-49, "And why call ye Me, 'Lord, Lord,' and do not the things which I say? Whosoever cometh to Me, and heareth My sayings and doeth them, I will show you to whom he is like: He is like a man who built a house and dug deep and laid the foundation on a rock; and when the flood arose, the stream beat vehemently upon that house and could not shake it, for it was founded upon a rock. But he that heareth, and doeth not, is like a man that built a house without a foundation upon the earth, against which the stream beat vehemently, and immediately it fell. And the ruin of that house was great."

One of my desires in ministry is to teach, train, and equip believers to be certain they have dug deep and secured themselves on the Rock—that entails having an understanding of the firm foundation found in Truth.

What is the goal of B.A.S.I.C. Training? There are basic teachings that happen to be extremely important issues we all should be discipled in after conceiving God's life. These things help us to develop and grow. I'm going to be dealing with some of those foundations in this book. There are many other areas in the Christian walk that are equally important to learn and understand, but the topics I'm going to discuss are some of the basics that will ensure your survival in the spiritual war going on in this world, the war you probably didn't know you were enlisted to fight in when you knelt before God.

BECOMING

PART ONE

What are you becoming? What goals do you have in your life? When you set a goal in your life to become something, are you automatically what you desire to be? Or do you have to go through a process before you achieve what you set out to accomplish?

If you set a goal to become a doctor, you must attend college and medical school and **complete** them before you become a doctor. You're not automatically a medical doctor just because you were accepted into medical school. There are many different things you must learn: human anatomy, the way the body functions, microbiology, which medications are administered to fight certain illnesses, etc. There are multiple exams you must pass before they will give you a diploma.

Because of Adam, we all come into this world in a fallen state. We have a sin nature at birth. We need a savior, someone to redeem us from that fallen nature. We are lost, and we need someone to find us. Jesus came for this purpose. He was the second Adam, the one whose purpose was to fulfill the law and pay the price for sin. The price for the sin that entered the world through the first Adam was death. Jesus took all the sin upon Himself and died, but He rose again victorious over it, passing on to those who believe the power to overcome as well.

When we hear the gospel (the good news that He paid the price for us) and believe it, He breathes upon us, imparting His Spirit, His Life, and His Light into us. That initial moment, when we have that experience with God and He breathes upon us, is conceiving the life of God. His Spirit enters our spirit and covers us with His blood in much the same way as when a woman conceives life. The sperm fertilizes the egg, the fertilized egg implants in the lining of blood in the uterus, and life is conceived. Were it not for the covering of the blood, His Spirit would not impart life because the life is in the blood. **(Leviticus 17:11)**

Once you have conceived the life of God, you have set out on an adventure walking through this world with God. You have started on this path, but you have not come to the end of the journey. You have yet to cross the finish line. You have started a growing process, but you are not yet fully grown. You have begun training, but you have not yet graduated. There are things you have to actually do when you follow after Jesus. Yes, you are saved by grace through faith, and it is not a result of works or working for God's approval, but faith without works is dead. **(James 2:20)**

Salvation is not a decision you make; salvation is not a prayer you say; salvation **is** a birthing, and births take time. In a natural birth things have to grow and develop in order for that life to be transformed from a tiny person (one that doesn't resemble a human in the beginning) into a baby ready to enter a new world. Immediately after being conceived in the womb—in order for them to be ready to take on the world—changes have to take place. A brain, a heart, lungs, arms, legs, and many other things have to grow and develop. In the same way that the baby looks nothing like a person when it embeds in the blood-lining, we look nothing like Christ when we first embed in His blood. Natural and supernatural things take place when you are implanted into the kingdom of God, His realm.

Once you have conceived the life of God, this is your goal:

Ephesians 4:13, "Until we all come into the unity of the faith and of the knowledge of the Son of God, and **become** perfect men, unto the measure of the stature of the fullness of Christ."

This is our goal as Believers: to become a perfect man, to attain to the measure of the stature of the fullness of Christ. In other words, we want to be formed into His image.

How do we know that this is a process and not something that just magically happens when we receive Christ? How do we know that the work is not complete when we first conceived His Life within us? Remember what I said about that baby? In the beginning of development babies do not look like they will look after they develop, grow, and mature.

Philippians 3:12, "It is not as though I had **already attained it**, nor were already **perfect**; but I follow after, that I may seize hold of that for which Christ Jesus also seized hold of me."

The Apostle Paul said that he had not already attained it. He was not yet perfect, but he worked toward being perfect. He told us he wanted to seize hold of that which Jesus seized hold of him for. What does that mean? Jesus seized hold of Paul for a purpose. That purpose was to **become** a perfect man. Paul told us he worked toward that daily. Jesus seized us for the same purpose.

Galatians 4:19, "My little children, over whom I travail in birth again **until** Christ be formed in you."

Paul said here that he prayed for the Galatians continuously until they were formed into the image of Christ. This makes it clear that Christ was not yet formed completely in the Galatians, but He was **being** formed in them, and Paul was travailing in birth until this came to pass.

Prayer is part of what forms us into God's image. Did you get that? Paul birthed them, discipled them, and prayed for them. Someone else said something about a spiritual birth.

John 3:3, "Jesus answered and said unto him, 'Verily, verily I say unto thee, except a man be born again, he cannot see the Kingdom of God.' "

Jesus told Nicodemus he had to be born again. A birthing must take place in order to see the Kingdom of God. Paul travails in birth on behalf of the Galatians. The Galatians were Christians, but they were still being formed. They were **becoming**.

How do we know that the spiritual birth is a process that must be seen through to the end in order to receive the completed work of salvation?

Paul, in the book of Hebrews, speaking of angels says this. "Are they not all ministering spirits, sent forth to minister for those who **shall be** heirs of Salvation?"

This word shall is a future tense word. It is not that they had already obtained it, but they **shall** obtain it. Let me interject something right here. I am not saying believers have not received the life of God, nor am I saying they remain lost. Believers have been found, and God's life is imparted unto them for a purpose—to lead and guide them through this world and the spiritual journey of becoming, but it is a process. As B. H. Clendennen always said, "We are saved and being saved."

Again in **Hebrews 3:6** Paul says, "But Christ was faithful as a son over his own house, whose house are we **if** we hold fast the confidence and rejoicing of the hope, **firm unto the end**."

You see, Paul makes it very clear to us that complete salvation is something that we receive in the end if we hold firm. That word **if** is a small word, but it is a powerful word. It implies a stipulation. There are stipulations when it comes to being a believer. We have to hold fast. The Greek word for fast means: to keep in memory, to possess, to retain, and to seize on.

We have to keep in memory the confidence and rejoicing of the hope. We have to possess the confidence and rejoicing of the hope. We have to retain the confidence and rejoicing of the hope. We have to seize the confidence and rejoicing of the hope. What hope is this? It is our expectation and confidence in Him as our deliverer. We have to believe more than that he simply He died for our sins. We have to believe His death and resurrection gives us the power to become.

What is it that we are to become? We are to become the Image of Jesus. That means we are to act like Jesus, respond like Jesus, and do the things Jesus did, including the miracles. Jesus Himself said we would do greater things than He did. **(John 14:12)**

1. Have you conceived the Life of God? Have you had an experience with Him that changed your life? Do you remember when you had that experience?
2. Are you seeking to become a perfect man? In other words, are you moving forward with allowing God to form you into His image? He will do the work. We can't, but we must allow Him to do it. In this way we are co-workers with Him.
3. Have you had the mindset that you've already attained all there is to attain?
4. Are you holding fast? In other words are you keeping in memory your confidence in the hope that He completed the work necessary for your salvation? Are you possessing that confidence, seizing hold of it?

Ponder these things over the next week and examine your heart.

BECOMING

PART TWO

After you have started this training process, there are some things that you must do. Trust me, it's a training process; it's a discipline. That's why we are called Disciples of Christ. We are going to look at some of these things right now.

To begin, how do we know that there are things we **must** do?

Philippians 2:12, "Therefore, my beloved, as ye have always obeyed, not only in my presence, but now much more in my absence, **work out** your own salvation with fear and trembling."

There are things we must work out concerning our salvation. Paul said to do so with fear and trembling. That word fear literally means alarm, fright, fear, and terror, yet it also comes from a root word meaning to hold onto, to possess, and the word trembling means quaking with fear. We normally don't like to imagine there is a place for those kinds of feelings in our walk with God, but according to the Apostle Paul, there is when it comes to working out our salvation.

There are things that must be done.

YOU MUST:

Retrain your mind: What kind of mind are you supposed to have?

I Corinthians 2:16, "For who hath known the mind of the Lord, that he may instruct him? But we have the **mind** of Christ."

How do you attain the mind of Christ?

Romans 12:2, "And be not conformed to this world, but be ye transformed by the renewing of your mind, that ye may prove what is that good and acceptable and perfect will of God."

We are transformed into the image of Christ by renewing our minds, but how do we accomplish that?

Ephesians 5:26, "That He might sanctify and cleanse it (the church) with the washing of water by the Word."

Our minds are renewed when we wash them with the water of God's Word. We came into this world with a sin nature as I stated in the last chapter. Our minds were infiltrated with darkness. Don't believe me? Little children will automatically do things they are not supposed to do. They have to be taught **not** to do certain things. Go ahead, set out a plate of cookies and tell them not to touch them. They will wait until mom is not looking and sneak one. When you ask them if they got into the cookies, despite the fact that you can see the evidence on their little

13

faces, they will automatically lie to keep out of trouble. You do not have to teach children to do wrong. It is already in their nature. You have to teach them to do right.

I would like to make a point here. As a parent God has taught me not to be angry with my children when they do wrong—not that I'm perfect and haven't gotten angry when I shouldn't because trust me, I have. But He's teaching me through my children to see their mistakes as an opportunity to give instruction.

Those with the sin nature are going to sin. We should expect it. Our children are going to do wrong and make mistakes, we should expect it and handle them with the same grace that God has shown us. Are there consequences for those mistakes? Yes, there are, but we should deal out those consequences in love and not in anger. In this way we are an example to our children of how God deals with His children. He disciplines in love.

Our minds are full of darkness by the time we come to Christ and that darkness must be cleansed.

When you take a bath, the water cleanses your body. In the same manner, when you read the word of God and apply it to your heart and life, it will cleanse your mind. Through the washing of the Word, we are able to change our minds to see things the way God sees them. The Word tells us the kind of things we should think on.

What kind of things does the Word of God tell us to think on?

Philippians 4:8, "Finally, brethren, whatsoever things are true, whatsoever things are honest, whatsoever things are just, whatsoever things are pure, whatsoever things are lovely, whatsoever things are of a good report; if there be any virtue and if there be any praise, think on these things."

If we strive to fill our minds with things that fall in these categories, then the filth of the world can be cleansed from our minds and no longer have place in our hearts or minds, and it's not just the filth of the world that is cleansed; it is the lies of the world that is cleansed from our minds. The world will tell you that you're nobody, but as the Word of God washes your mind of that lie, you will see yourself the way God sees you!

Is that it? Is that all we have to do? Do we clean our minds and that's the end of the story? No!

YOU MUST:

Subdue your body. How do we know that God wants us to subdue our body?

Genesis 1:28, "And God blessed them, and God said unto them, 'Be fruitful and multiply, and replenish the earth, and subdue it.'"

God gave man and woman dominion over everything in the earth, including our own bodies.

I Thessalonians 5:23, "And the very God of peace sanctify you wholly; and I pray

God your whole spirit and soul and body be preserved blameless unto the coming of our Lord Jesus Christ."

Paul says that God will sanctify us wholly. He says that our body should be preserved blameless. This makes it clear that we have to deal with some things concerning our body.

What does it mean to subdue your body? It means that you bring your body (your flesh) into subjection to your spirit. Your spirit should control your body, your flesh.

How do you control your flesh?

Galatians 5:16 and 17, "This I say then: Walk in the Spirit, and ye shall not fulfill the lust of the flesh. For the flesh lusteth against the Spirit, and the Spirit against the flesh; and these are contrary the one to the other, so that ye cannot do the things that ye would."

If we walk in the Spirit, we will not fulfill the lust of the flesh, so how do we walk in the Spirit?

Romans 13:14, "But put ye on the Lord Jesus Christ, and make not provision for the flesh to fulfill the lusts thereof."

We have to put on Jesus, his mindset. We do this by cleansing our minds to be like Him and no longer making opportunity for the flesh. Do not open the door for sin in the flesh. When the temptation comes, flee from it. It is not always easy, but the Word of God assures us that if we call upon Him, He will make a way of escape.

Sometimes we must die to what we may want if the thing we want is sin.

Galatians 5:24, "And those who are Christ's **have crucified** the flesh with its affections and lusts."

When you crucify something, you put it to death. This is not pleasant. Your body or flesh may really want to do the thing that the Word is telling you not to do.

So, what happens if we don't subdue our body and bring it into subjection to our spirit?

Galatians 6:8, "For he that soweth to his flesh shall of the flesh reap corruption; but he that soweth to the Spirit shall of the Spirit reap life everlasting."

You reap corruption if you sow to the flesh. You only reap life everlasting if you sow to the Spirit.

So, what is this corruption spoken of?

Romans 8:13, "For if ye live according to the flesh **ye shall die**, but if ye through the Spirit do mortify the deeds of the body ye shall live."

Now, we know this death is not a physical death but a spiritual one because we will all die a physical death on this earth, but if we mortify (put to death) the deeds of the body through the Spirit, we will live.

Romans 12:1, "I beseech you therefore, brethren, by the mercies of God, that ye present your bodies a living sacrifice, holy, acceptable unto God, which is your reasonable service."

God wants us to keep our bodies holy. This is what is acceptable to Him. Paul tells us that this is a reasonable thing. It is not too difficult to do. It is reasonable.

1. Are you working out your salvation with fear and trembling as the Apostle Paul says you should?

2. Are you retraining your mind by washing it with the water of the Word?

3. What are you becoming? Are you becoming a person whose thoughts are consumed with the Word? Or are you becoming a person whose thoughts are overtaken with the darkness of the world?

4. Are you becoming a person who is ruled by the flesh, the wants and desires of your body? Or are you becoming a person who is working to put your body into subjection to your spirit.

ARMED

PART ONE

Once you've answered the questions from the previous two weeks and determined if you are indeed on the path of becoming what God has called you to be (a reflection of Him), it is time to learn about the war going on all around you—the war you were drafted into the moment you submitted to God and received His Life within you. You have an enemy; he seeks to destroy you, but God has supplied you with the things needed to battle him.

I Timothy 1:18 and19, "This charge I commit unto thee, son Timothy, according to the prophecies which went before concerning thee, that thou by them mightiest wage a good warfare, holding faith and a good conscience, which some having put aside, have suffered shipwreck concerning faith."

You might be wondering why you need to be armed. I mean after all, wasn't Jesus peaceful? Didn't He come to bring peace on earth and goodwill to men? That's what we've always been told, so why arm ourselves? Why do we need armor if He came to bring peace?

The answer to that is yes; Jesus was a peaceful man, but He, Himself—by his own admission—did not come to bring peace on earth. It was the angels who appeared to the shepherds who declared 'and on earth peace, good will toward men.' **(Luke 2:14)** They were praising God for His desire and plan to bring rest to mankind and set at one again the unity, communion, and fellowship between humanity and God through the birth of the Word. The Greek word for peace here comes from a root verb that means to join. God Himself joined humanity that night in the form of a baby.

Jesus declares in **Matthew 10:34**, "Think not that I am come to send peace on earth. I came not to send peace, but a sword."

He came to bring a sword. Why? Because we are in a war!

This section will talk about what that war is and how we should arm ourselves, but first, let me ask you this: What do you think your chances of survival would be if you went out into warfare without any armor? Very slim, I assure you. Ask any of our soldiers or vets who have been in war. If you are not properly protected with a way to take out the enemy, your chances of making it out of the jungles or the deserts or wherever you happen to be fighting are almost nonexistent.

So, here's the next set of questions. If we are in a war, who called us to this war? Who or what is it that we are fighting for in this war?

Numbers 32:20-23, "And Moses said unto them, 'If ye will do this thing, if ye will go armed before the Lord to war, and will go all of you armed over the Jordan before the Lord, until He hath driven out His enemies from before Him and the land be subdued before the Lord, then afterward ye shall return and be guiltless before the Lord and before Israel (the Church) and this land shall be your possession before the Lord. But if ye will not do so, behold, ye have sinned against the Lord; and be sure your sin will find you out.' "

Moses let us know that the Lord Himself is the one who has called us to this war. We are to go before Him, and He will drive out the enemies. There may be those of you reading this thinking to yourself, *That was old testament; we are living in the new testament. How can that be applied?*

True, that was an Old Testament scripture of a literal war the Lord called the children of Israel into, but being under the new covenant does not negate the spiritual truths we learn and glean from the old. Go back and read **I Timothy 1:18 and 19**. The Apostle Paul wrote to Timothy and charged him to wage a good warfare. That's New Testament proof we're in a war. Paul also told Timothy how to wage a good warfare, to hold faith and a good conscience. We also see in that scripture the result of not doing those things, but we'll get into that a little later. We know according to Paul that we as believers are in a war, and guess what; Jesus came to send out swords to those who would join Him in the battle!

What is it we are fighting for? We are fighting to possess the Land. What is this land? There are two lands we are to possess. They are both spiritual lands. The first land we are to possess lies within us, the second outside of us. I'll get into how we go about possessing the land outside of us after I talk about the spiritual land within us we must conquer first.

SPIRITUAL LANDS

THE TEMPLE

I Corinthians 3:16, "Know ye not that ye are the temple of God, and that the Spirit of God dwelleth in you?"

Our bodies are the temple of God Almighty; therefore, we must take possession of it. What do I mean by that? Am I saying that you did not already possess your own body? We are triune beings, just as God is a triune being. We were created like Him in that way. We have a body; we have a soul, and we have a spirit. Our spirits were meant to be in control of our body and soul, but sadly, that is not the case when we come to God.

Luke 21:19, "In your patience possess ye your souls."

We are instructed to possess our souls. This did not automatically happen when we first conceived God's Life. No one bows their knee to God for the first time and stands up with their spirit completely in control of their mind, their will, their emotions, or their flesh. It is a journey the Holy Spirit will lead us into.

I Thessalonians 5:23, "And the very God of peace sanctify you wholly; and I pray God your whole spirit and soul and body be preserved blameless unto the coming of our Lord Jesus Christ."

I'm well aware that we looked at I Thessalonians in the second chapter, but the same applies here as well. We must first possess our souls, our mind, our will, and our emotions, and in doing so we subdue our bodies, bringing them into subjection to our spirit. This is our land that we must arm ourselves to conquer, the first land we must conquer before going forward to conquer the world.

What is our reward for obeying, arming ourselves, and doing what God has commanded us to do? Moses told us that afterward we will be guiltless before the Lord and before Israel (which is a type of the Church) and the land (our souls and our flesh) will be our possession. So, what does that mean? It means that our spirit will be the one in control of our mind, our will, our emotions, and our flesh.

SCENARIO:

A war. The enemy has total control over the entire country (Your mind, your will, your emotions, and your flesh before you conceived the life of God). Allied soldiers swoop in and begin to take possession of the land. They don't take the entire land all at once. They progress. They conquer one part and then move on to the next area, seeking to take control back from the enemy. **(Exodus 23:30)**

The allied soldier who swoops in and leads you to take possession is the Holy Spirit. He drives the enemies out little by little. As He guides you into the areas of your life the enemy has control over, you must submit your spirit to Him to take back that territory from the enemy. Once your spirit, after being made alive by the Holy Spirit, subdues your soul and flesh; then you will be guiltless and possess (have control over) your own soul and body.

Who is it we are at war with? Who is our enemy?

Revelation 12:17, "And the dragon was wroth with the woman, and he went to make war with the remnant of her seed, who keep the commandments of God, and have the testimony of Jesus Christ."

Do you have the testimony of Jesus Christ? Do you keep the commandments of God? If so, then you are at war with the dragon! It doesn't matter if you want to be in a war or not; you are in a war by default because the dragon went to make war with the remnant.

So, who exactly is this dragon?

Revelation 12:9, "And the great dragon was cast out—that serpent of old called the Devil and Satan, who deceiveth the whole world. He was cast out onto the earth, and his angels were cast out with him."

The great dragon is none other than Satan. You and I are at war with Satan and the fallen angels who are known as demons. One of the lies that the enemy has successfully infiltrated the world with is that he is not real. He is very real, and for those who have enough spiritual understanding to recognize he is in fact real, he convinces them that he is in Hell. **(Job 2:2)** Satan is not bound in Hell; he roams the earth as a roaring lion, seeking to devour. **(I Peter 5:8)**

Now that you know you are in a real war, a war going on around you in the spiritual realm, it is important to know how to equip yourself to battle the enemy seeking to destroy you.

In war there are those who are offensive (invading) and there are those who are defensive (protecting). You must arm yourselves to fight in both manners.

DEFENSIVE:

Luke 11:21 and 22, "When a strong man armed keepeth his palace, his goods are in peace. But when one stronger than he shall come upon him and overcome him, he taketh from him all his armor wherein he trusted, and divideth his spoils."

We must arm ourselves to protect and defend our souls. The enemy will be constantly attacking us personally. We must defend the territory already taken control of by us during battle. We are not to rebuild those things which we have already destroyed. When you take possession of your own mind, your own will, your own emotions, your own flesh, do not rebuild those things you have conquered. When we keep our palace (our soul), we have peace. We can trust in our armor, but if we do not utilize our armor and if we attempt to fight the enemy through our own strength, he will overcome us and take that armor from us.

Pointer: If you happen to notice that you've lost peace—you're feeling worry and turmoil—examine yourself to see if the enemy has invaded. It just may be that he has and you didn't use what God has taught you in order to keep the enemy out. We've all done it; we've all let our guard down. Recognizing we've allowed the enemy in by not being on guard is the first step to getting him out and regaining peace and getting back what he took from us.

Do not deceive yourself. In your own strength, you cannot stand against Satan. He is more powerful, but Jesus overcame him, and when you utilize His power and strength, Satan cannot stand against you!

OFFENSIVE:

2 Corinthians 10:4-5, "For the weapons of our warfare are not carnal, but mighty through God for the pulling down of strongholds, casting down imaginations and every high thing that exalteth itself against the knowledge of God, and bringing into captivity every thought to the obedience of Christ."

You see, our weapon is not a natural weapon. We don't go around toting guns demanding that the evil people who run this world submit to us. Our weapons are mighty through God. We must invade first the territory of our own heart, our own soul, our own will, our own minds, our own emotions, and our own flesh that the enemy may still have control over and take it away from him.

We have to tear down their strongholds. What are strongholds, you ask? Strongholds are places that are fortified, places easily defended and less susceptible to attack, places that have been strengthened and reinforced. The enemy has strongholds— places they feel safe because they've strengthened them, fortified them, and reinforced them—within us and within the world, but through God we can and **must** pull those places down and cast down the thoughts and imaginations that exalt themselves against the knowledge of God.

We must bring those things into **our** captivity, under the subjection of our spirit, and into the obedience of Christ. The thoughts placed in our minds that go against the Word, take them captive and bring them down by combating them with what the Word says.

Matthew 16:19, "And I will give unto thee the keys of the Kingdom of Heaven. And whatsoever thou shalt bind on earth shall be bound in Heaven, and whatsoever thou shalt loose on earth shall be loosed in Heaven."

This is our weapon. We have the authority to bind the demonic forces that have infiltrated this world. We have the authority to loose the minds of those bound by them. This is done through prayer.

THE KINGDOM

James 2:5, "Hearken, my beloved brethren: Hath not God chosen the poor of this world, rich in faith, to be heirs of the Kingdom which He hath promised to those who love Him?"

We are promised a kingdom, so what is this kingdom and where is it? How do we obtain this Kingdom that was promised to us?

Colossians 1:13, "He hath delivered us from the power of darkness, and hath translated us into the Kingdom of His dear Son."

Wow! Do you realize it is a supernatural event that has taken place? God delivered us from the darkness of this world, a world ruled by the prince of darkness, and translated us into the Kingdom of Jesus. His Kingdom is a Kingdom of light.

Mark 4:11, "...Unto you (disciples) it is given to know the mystery of the Kingdom of God; but unto them that are without, all these things are done in parables."

We know there is a mystery concerning the Kingdom of God, but we as believers are given the ability to know what that mystery is. So, what is that mystery revealed? Where is the Kingdom of God? And what is it?

Luke 17:21, "Neither shall they say, 'Lo it is here!' or 'Lo it is there' (speaking of the Kingdom of God) for behold, the Kingdom of God is within you."

The Kingdom of God is within us as believers! Meditate on that for a minute… That is awesome news from a Mighty God. Not only did God supernaturally translate us into His Kingdom, but He placed His Kingdom within us! So, what exactly is this Kingdom within us, and what is it doing there? What's its purpose?

I Corinthians 4:20, "For the Kingdom of God is not in word, but in power."

The Kingdom within us is power. It is the power of Light and Truth that can and will dispel the darkness engulfing this world. We are meant to be carriers of this Light, Truth, and power—warriors who invade the darkness that has consumed this world, the second land we are meant to possess. What's the purpose of this Kingdom within us? What's the purpose of this power within us?

Luke 10:19, "Behold, I give unto you power to tread on serpents and scorpions and over all the power of the enemy, and nothing by any means shall hurt you."

The word used here for serpents is not speaking of a literal snake. It is referring to a figurative snake, especially Satan. It can be a malicious person. The word for scorpion means to pierce from its sting. Its base word means concealment, a watch, or a scout. These are spiritual beings, minions of the devil and even the devil himself that we are given power to tread upon. They are malicious; they conceal themselves in the darkness of this world, watching and scouting out because they are an army bent on keeping this world in darkness, but we have been given the power to defeat them!

Now, let's go back and look at what I mentioned in the beginning of this section. There were results of not doing as Paul instructed Timothy concerning waging a good warfare. Some had not done so and suffered shipwreck. That word for shipwreck is derived from two words, one meaning to become a fool, to be made foolish, to lose savour. They had put aside faith and a good conscience and became fools.

If we do not wage war with the enemy, if we turn our back on it, if we are not defensive as well as offensive, we risk suffering shipwreck.

1. Have you gone into warfare without any armor? If you have, your chances of survival are almost non-existent.

2. Have you been battling to possess your own soul?

3. Have you joined the rest of the army to battle the darkness invading the rest of the world?

4. Do you recognize the enemy?

5. Are your goods, your soul, in peace?

6. Have you been trying to use natural weapons to fight a supernatural enemy?

7. Have you recognized the mystery of the Kingdom of God? Do you have an understanding that the Kingdom is within you?

8. Do you understand that the Kingdom within you is power to defeat the enemy that has this world in bondage?

ARMED

PART TWO

Ephesians 6: 10-12, "Finally, my brethren, be strong in the Lord and in the power of His might. Put on the whole armor of God, that ye may be able to stand against the wiles of the devil. For we wrestle not against flesh and blood, but against principalities, against powers, against the rulers of darkness of this world, against spiritual wickedness in high places."

We are called into a war, but our war is not with mortals. If you step out into the darkness of this world and you try to wrestle

41

and fight against mere mortals (those consumed by the darkness), you will not prevail, and you will have accomplished nothing for the Kingdom. Take down one wicked mortal, and another will take his place. We've seen that all throughout history. Take down the principality who gave the wicked mortal his strength to inflict this world with darkness, and the mortal is merely a mortal without power.

Our power is a supernatural power meant to battle against supernatural beings. The lost world is not our enemy. The lost people within it are not our enemies. For too long Satan has defeated the church by causing us to look at the people he has used rather than seeing the demonic forces that are controlling them.

If we are in a war with supernatural beings and need to be armed for that war, what is the armor that we should have? According to Paul in Ephesians, we should put on armor—the whole armor. Why? So we can stand against the darkness. This means, if we do not put on the whole armor, we will not be able to stand against the enemy, so it is crucial to know what this armor is.

Romans 13:12, "The night is far spent; the day is at hand. Let us therefore cast off the works of darkness, and let us put on the armor of light."

First, we must cast off the darkness on us. Don't fool yourself into thinking works of darkness are not on you. They are the works of the flesh. So, what are they?

Galatians 5:19-21, "Now the works of the flesh are manifest, and they are these: adultery, fornication, uncleanness, lasciviousness, idolatry, witchcraft, hatred, quarreling, rivalry, wrath, strife, seditions, heresies, envying, murders, drunkenness, revelings, and such like. About these things I tell you again, as I have also told you in times past: that those who do such things shall not inherit the Kingdom of God."

Okay, so maybe you can say with all confidence that you don't practice witchcraft, and you're not an adulterer. What is an adulterer? Jesus said if a man looks upon a woman to lust after her, he has committed adultery in his heart. A large percentage of the divorces in this country are a result of such a thing, men unable to refrain from watching videos and looking at pictures of another woman. It is bondage; it is a work of darkness, and you need to be freed from it. It will destroy your marriage.

What about hatred and envy? People do things to hurt us or our children, and we get angry. It's normal, but when that anger goes unchecked, it can turn to hatred, and it is a work of darkness. We must cast it off and forgive. Forgiveness does not mean what was done was okay, it means you let it go and allow God to be your defender. It's not always easy, but it can be done.

Do you like your neighbor's house? Do you want it so much that it consumes you? Am I saying it's wrong to want a nice home? No, I'm not, but wanting something just because someone else has it—that is wrong.

The works of darkness are constantly bombarding us to try and find a place in our heart so that we cannot put on the armor of light. So, what is the armor of light?

Ephesians 6:14-17, "Stand therefore, having your loins girded about with truth, and having on the breastplate of righteousness, and your feet shod with the preparation of the gospel of peace. Above all, take the shield of faith, wherewith ye shall be able to quench all the fiery darts of the wicked. And take the helmet of salvation and the sword of the Spirit, which is the word of God."

THE ARMOR OF LIGHT

LOINS GIRDED

The word girded means to attach with a belt. The loins are from the hips down and include the genitals. This is the most vulnerable area of the body. Think about it, your brain is protected by your skull; your heart and lungs are protected by your ribs, but the groin area is left unprotected.

The word used for loins not only means the physical area, but it also means the procreative power, the power to reproduce. As believers we have the ability to plant seeds in the hearts and lives of unbelievers, and we do this by speaking Truth.

The belt that Roman soldiers wore was a metal belt called a cingulim. From the belt hung decorated leather strips that protected the groin in battle. The noise it created assisted in intimidating the enemy. It was used to hold the breastplate on and in place, and it was also where the weapons were kept.

Our belt is Truth. The physical belt gave strength and protection to the weak areas of the body, and Truth gives strength to the weak areas of our spiritual body. It is Truth that holds the breastplate on and in place. It is the Truth we carry into battle that intimidates the enemy. Truth protects our ability to convert the lost world, and Truth holds our offensive weapon.

Why do we need Truth to protect our procreative power? **(Revelation 12:9)** Satan has the world deceived, and he seeks to deceive even the believer. We are warned repeatedly not to be deceived; therefore, we can be deceived. Knowing the Truth protects us from deception, and in turn it protects the seeds we are to plant in the hearts of the unbelievers. Truth is what frees them from their bondage.

Why do we need Truth to hold our breastplate in place? **(2 Timothy 3:16)** Truth gives us correction, reproof, and instructions in righteousness.

Why do we need Truth to intimidate the enemy? **(2 Timothy 2: 24-26)** Truth exposes the lies the enemy has used to ensnare those he holds captive. He is intimidated when faced with Truth. He knows the Word and will twist it, but when faced with someone knowing unadulterated Truth, he flees.

Why do we need Truth to hold our offensive weapon? **(John 8:44)** Satan is the father of lies. Truth holds the sword of the Spirit, the

Word of God that exposes and defeats his lies. The two are joined at the hip, if you will. Combine Truth with the power of His Spirit, and Satan cannot win.

BREASTPLATE

The breastplate was only used in battle. It was made of leather with metal to protect the chest area. This part of the armor secures the vital organs. The heart and the lungs are those vital organs. Our breastplate is righteousness. There are two aspects of righteousness, just as the breastplate is made of both metal and leather.

The first aspect is: We have the righteousness of Christ. **(Philippians 3:9)** Our own righteousness serves little purpose. Apart from faith in Jesus and His righteousness, our righteousness is as filthy rags, yet righteousness means doing what is right in God's eyes. The second aspect is: We have a part that we are expected to fulfill. How do we do this? The Word of God tells us that God writes His laws on our hearts. You see, it is Jesus' righteousness that is placed in your heart by God when you conceive His Life. He writes on our hearts what is right in His eyes, His laws. With His laws written upon our hearts, we can do what is right in His eyes by allowing Him to live through us.

The heart is what pumps your blood through your veins. The job of blood is to cleanse, to carry oxygen, and to bring life. The heart works in conjunction with the lungs. The lungs provide the oxygen needed by your body to the heart so that it may be delivered to the rest of the body. Your every breath is protected through righteousness.

His laws being written on your heart to do righteousness is what makes the blood of Jesus flow through your life. It pumps His blood through your body. It cleanses you by carrying waste products (sin) to be eliminated from the body. It carries the oxygen (the Spirit of God) through the body, bringing you God's life.

(Revelation 12:10) tells us that Satan is the accuser of the brethren. He was cast onto the earth, and he roams about accusing us of past sins and present failures.

So, how do we use the breastplate in battle with the enemy? **(1 John 1:9)** When we're in the midst of the battle and the enemy comes to accuse and make us feel we can't take another step forward, we confess our sins, and Jesus will cleanse us from the unrighteousness. His blood will flow through and eliminate the waste product of sin. Satan's arrows cannot penetrate the righteousness of Jesus, and it cannot pierce through His forgiveness either.

FEET SHOD

The shoes that soldiers wore were an important part of preparation for battle. These shoes were made of leather and had hobnails in the soles for traction. The thick soles served to protect the feet, and the hobnails gave them the ability to advance uphill in the worst weather. They also kept the soldier from being distracted by anything they might step on in battle.

Your shoes are the preparation of the gospel of peace. They represent our call to take the good news of Jesus to the world. **(Matt 28:16-20)** We have been commissioned by Jesus to go into the world and make disciples. Why the preparation of the gospel? The word for preparation literally means to make ready. You must be prepared, prepared for the battle and prepared to deliver the good news. You cannot go marching into enemy territory (that is, after all, where the gospel needs to be taken) without preparation or training. If you are not adequately prepared for the spiritual battle that you are in, you may fall into a trap, or you may be easily distracted during the battle and lose ground.

Proverbs 3:21-23, "My son, let not these depart from thine eyes: keep sound wisdom and discretion; so shall they be life unto thy soul, and grace around thy neck. Then shalt thou walk in thy way safely, and thy foot shall not stumble."

The word discretion in the original Hebrew means a plan. Part of our preparation and training is gaining wisdom and making a plan. These things will keep our feet from stumbling.

SHIELD

The Roman soldiers' shields were made of wood, covered in leather. The soldiers would wet the leather before battle so they could quench the fiery darts of the enemy. The army would hold their shields in front of them as they stood in a line and then soldiers would line up behind them and hold the shields up overhead. This would make it almost impossible for them to be hit by a fiery dart. The wetness of the shield would put out the fire.

Our shield is faith. Faith is the most important part of our armor. Faith will be your all in all in the hour of temptation. Place faith between you and the arrows of the enemy, and the fire will be quenched, and the arrow will not penetrate. So, how do we gain this faith?

Romans 10:17 and Jude 1:20.

First, we gain faith by hearing the Word of God, and secondly, we build upon that faith by praying in the Holy Ghost.

So, how do we use the shield of faith? The enemy will come and bring doubt about the Word of God, attempting to convince you that God will not do what He said in His Word. Satan will try to convince you the Word is a lie, and he will do his best to twist the Word and deceive you.

When he comes, lift the shield by praying for God to help your unbelief. Confess the Truth of scripture when the devil says it's a lie. Study the Word and rightly divide it so you can stand on Truth when Satan attempts to twist it.

SIDE NOTE: notice that armies went to battle together so that they were completely shielded. A lone soldier would not be able to do that.

HELMET

The helmet was only worn in battle as well. It protected the head. The head houses the command center of our bodies, the brain. It is the most amazing super-computer in existence, telling our lungs to breathe without a thought, telling our heart to beat without a thought, and commanding our movements as it quickly thinks through how we should or should not react to any given situation. Without it, we are a lifeless lump of bones, muscles, and skin holding everything else together.

Our helmet is salvation, and it protects our minds. The Greek word used for salvation means defender, and it comes from a word that means rescue, safety, deliver, health, salvation, and the root word to both of them means deliverer! Our hope of salvation—defense, rescue, safety, deliverance, health, and ultimate salvation—will protect our mind from the words of the enemy.

If we fill our minds and guard our minds with the promises of the Word of God, we will have the defenses we need to ward off the negative words of the enemy (those words that do not line up with God's Word, the half-truths and the deceptions Satan tries to plant in our heads) when he comes to speak lies.

So, what are those promises? He will be our defense; He will rescue us and provide a way of escape when needed; He is our safety under the shadow of His wings; He is our deliverance, delivering us from our enemies; He is our health and healing because by His stripes we were healed; and He is our ultimate salvation, seeing us through to the end and giving us His grace which is sufficient for us.

When we are wearing our helmets and the words of the enemy come and tell us: there is no hope; we have already lost the battle; it doesn't seem that God is defending us; He's allowing us to be slaughtered on the battlefield; He hasn't opened a door of escape or rescue; you're surely not safe; you're being beat down; God has forsaken you; healing? Yeah, right. Your body is riddled with pain and sickness. How can you say God has healed you? When those words come (if we have on our helmet of salvation), our minds are protected from his words. They cannot penetrate through the helmet

So, what happens if we take that helmet off? Our minds are fair game for the enemy. He will come in like a flood, bombarding our every thought, and unless we put that helmet back on, we will not survive his attack. He will convince us of those things he is whispering to us—sometimes screaming them at us. He will persuade us we have been left to die alone at the hands of our enemies.

SWORD

The sword was used in close battle. Paul only mentions the use of this offensive weapon. He doesn't indicate the weapons that are used in far off battles. Why? I believe there is a reason. The battle we are in is close! The enemy is not far off attacking us. He gets in close, sometimes sending in wolves in sheep's clothing, and other times, sending in minions we can't see.

The sword is our offensive weapon, the sword of the Spirit, the Word of God. When you combine the power of the Spirit of God with the Word of God, the enemy will be defeated! When the enemy is before us, we can rise up and speak the Word of God back to the enemy. That is, after all, how Jesus defeated Satan. When Satan tried to twist the Word, Jesus spoke the Word back to him.

Remember, the breastplate is held on by Truth. If you do not know the Truth, your breastplate of righteousness will not stay on, and it protects the vital organs that send the breath of life through your body and the constant cleansing flow of Jesus' blood.

Did you happen to notice that in the description of all the armor, there is no armament for the back? Wonder why this is? If we ever turn our back on the enemy, then we are completely exposed. In other words, we can't ignore him and pretend he is not there. We have to be conscious of the war we are in, always moving forward.

Not many of us would dare turn our back on God, but how often are we frightened by the war or the battle we see lying before us, so we turn our back on the fight. We want to pretend it's not there at all. When we do that, we expose the only vulnerable part of us to the enemy, giving him the opportunity to pierce us in the back with one of his fiery darts. We aren't facing him, so we surely can't hold up our shield of faith. We don't even see the flames as they head for us and wound us. When we are moving forward in the battle, God is our rear guard. He has our back, but when we turn from the battle, He is no longer behind us to protect the vulnerable part of us.

We are meant to be an army, marching forward in the name of Jesus. What does that mean?

He is our King. Kings would send out their armies in their names. Their names represented their power and their status. We represent the King of kings and the Lord of lords. His power resides within us. We are His representatives. We are Christians; that's our status. The Greek word used for Christians is derived from the word that means anointed. We have been consecrated to an office, an office of a warrior on His behalf.

Isaiah 61:1-3, "The Spirit of the Lord God is upon Me, because the Lord hath anointed Me to preach good tidings unto the meek. He hath sent Me to bind up the brokenhearted, to proclaim liberty to the captives, and the opening of the prison to them that are bound, to proclaim the acceptable year of the Lord and the day of vengeance of our God, to comfort all that mourn, to appoint unto them that mourn in Zion, to give unto them beauty for ashes, the oil of joy for mourning, the garment of praise for the spirit of heaviness, that they might be called trees of righteousness, the planting of the Lord, that He might be glorified."

We have been anointed to do all these things. We are meant to charge forward onto the battlefield—getting up close and personal with the enemy of our souls, the enemy of the church, the enemy of the world—and use a weapon he and his demons cannot stand against, the Word of the Living God!

But know this, the armor that you must put on, that armor of light, it is personal. You must personally put on your armor. I can't put yours on for you. I can simply warn you it is needed, but the battle is a group effort. You cannot do it alone. A Roman soldier by himself was vulnerable, but as a unified army they were virtually invincible. You are vulnerable by yourself, but as a unified army with the rest of the body of Christ, we are an army that **IS** invincible! We cannot and we will not be defeated.

1. Do you have on your armor?

2. Have you prepared yourself for the spiritual battle that you are in? You're in it whether you like it or not. So, if you haven't prepared yourself, start right now.

3. What part of the armor are you missing?

4. Have you taken off your helmet, allowing the thoughts of the enemy to enter?

5. Have you left off the belt of Truth, the truths found in the Word of God, leaving your breastplate of righteousness falling to the ground at your feet and making you vulnerable to a lung or heart puncture? Truth and Righteousness work together. Remember that.

6. What about your shoes? Have you been walking on the battlefield barefoot, making yourself vulnerable to traps because you weren't adequately prepared to enter the battle? Discipleship is a necessary

part of the Christian walk. Don't give your life to God and go running into battle without being first taught the things you need to know in order to survive.

7. Have you dropped your shield of faith? Are you in need of the rest of God's army to come in and surround you, holding up their shields in front of you, over you, and behind you? There are times when this happens. We're injured in battle and drop our shield in the process. Our faith wanes, and we need our brothers and sisters to step in on our behalf and lift up their shields to protect us from the fiery darts of the enemy.

8. What about your sword? Have you left it in its sheath collecting dust? Grasp the hilt, pull it from its sheath, and thrust it into the heart of the enemy. It is double-edged. It will cut deep.

9. Have you kept yourself isolated from the rest of the army? You will not

survive the war, if you are not joined together with other soldiers, marching forward with a plan, a plan plotted out by God Himself and given to the leadership in your church.

SOLDIERS

PART ONE

You may be wondering, are we really soldiers? Maybe you thought Jesus did all the work on the cross and living a Christian life would mean peace and rest.

Jesus did do all of the work for your redemption, and a believer can and should have God's peace in the midst of all storms. Once we have been redeemed, we can rest from trying to work our way into heaven. Admit it, that's what most of us do before coming to Him and ceasing from our labors.

We try desperately to be "good enough." There's no longer any need for that, but there is a need to learn about the battle around you and to recognize that you are indeed a soldier.

Philippians 2:25, "Yet I have thought it necessary to send to you Epaphroditus, my brother and companion in labor and fellow soldier, who as your messenger ministered to my wants."

Paul referred to Epaphroditus as his brother, his companion, and his fellow soldier, meaning Paul was also a soldier. Are you a fellow soldier?

How did you or do you become a soldier? A soldier enlists. He or she signs up to be a soldier. When you converted (when the Life of God was conceived in you), you enlisted into God's army. If you happen to be reading this and you've never had the breath of Life breathed into your spirit, know this: accepting God means enlisting in His army.

Once a man or woman enlists in any of the branches of the military, they are sent to boot camp and given extensive training before being sent into battle. It is during this time the soldier is prepared for war. A good general does not and will not send an untrained man or woman into battle.

Two of the things you will learn in boot camp that are important for you to learn as one of God's soldiers are: Team work and military order.

TEAM WORK

We need each other. We can't do it alone. The military functions in order and in unity and so must we as the church.

MILITARY ORDER

This bit of information comes from how the Marines function. It is generalized information received from my daddy, a Marine.

Generals get together, look at a situation, and decide how they will attack the situation; they pass down their commands to the different Regiments under them, assigning them each with particular jobs spanning a particular location. The location may be vast and have many different things that need to be carried out over a wide distance.

The Regiments are made up of battalions. The battalions are then given their orders by the Regiments, breaking down the particular job given to that particular Regiment. One battalion may be sent into one region to deal with multiple issues while another battalion is sent into another region.

Battalions are made up of companies. The different companies are given their different orders based on the needs of the battalions, further breaking down what tasks need to be carried out in order to invade and take control over a province within a particular region.

Companies are made up of Platoons. The companies pass down specific orders to their various Platoons, further narrowing down their mission. Platoons are made up of Squads. Each squad within the Platoon is then given their orders, the assignments they are to carry out. They go in; they do what they were commanded; they take control over the territory that was once ruled by a dictator, and they fly their flag, showing victory!

Orders trickle down from the head; those who are able to see the whole picture and have the training to know what needs to be done to accomplish victory.

CHURCH ORDER

The Church has an order as well. We are a body, each having a different function. Jesus is the head, the commander. Our orders come down through him, being passed to the leadership established in the Word of God: Apostles, prophets, evangelists, pastors, and teachers.

EPHESIANS 4:11-12, "And He appointed some to be apostles, and some prophets, and some evangelists, and some pastors, and teachers, for the perfecting of the saints for the work of the ministry, and for the edifying of the body of Christ."

Those in leadership positions take their orders from God and pass down the vision given to them to the rest of the body. Now, there are some that don't like the idea of leadership within the body of Christ because they fear enslavement to a dictatorship by their pastor, and let's face it...it has happened. There have been false pastors, false teachers, and false prophets who have led people astray. That is why it is important to know the Truth, have that belt on, knowing what the Truth of the Word says.

If you find yourself within a body that is being misled by a false preacher, get out and find leadership not abusing its power. The fact that there have been false teachers and preachers does not change the fact that God still has an order in the church.

Each member of the body is given different gifts by God.

I Corinthians 12:4-11, "Now there are diversities of gifts, but the same Spirit. And there are differences of administrations, but the same Lord. And there are diversities of operations, but it is the same God who worketh all in all. But the manifestation of the Spirit is given to every man to profit withal: For to one is given by the Spirit the word of wisdom; to another the word of knowledge by the same Spirit; to another faith by the same Spirit; to another gifts of healing by the same Spirit; to another the working of miracles; to another prophecy; to another discerning of spirits; to another divers kinds of tongues; to another the interpretation of tongues. But all of these that one and the selfsame Spirit worketh, apportioning to every man individually as He will."

Jesus, the commander, sees the whole picture. He knows what needs to be done across the world to win the war. He also sees the whole picture in certain areas where churches exist. He passes down the instructions to the leadership within those churches, knowing what each church needs to do as a particular body.

The leadership of the church then receives the vision of how to wage warfare in their area as well as outlying areas the Lord wants that particular body to send missionaries to, and the leadership within the body passes on that vision to those who make up that body.

It takes the entire leadership to see the vision of the commander. There is a unity among them, but they each play a different part, much like the generals. They get together, discuss the instructions and the situations, and decide how best to attack and invade the enemy's territory. A pastor has a particular calling and sees his part in the vision, while the Apostle, the evangelist, the prophets, and the teachers each see their own part in the vision.

The body is made up of believers with a diversity of gifts given by the same Spirit.

These gifts are given to individuals to profit the entire body. Here is where it further breaks down into Regiments, battalions, companies, platoons, and squads. Of course, we don't call them by those names; we call them different ministries within the church. We have worship teams, Sunday Schools, discipleship classes, outreach ministries, prayer warriors, deliverance ministries, healing ministries, etc.

The gifts given to you by the Holy Spirit may enable you to work and function within different capacities. Squads are part of platoons, so you may be in a squad of deliverance ministries that is within a platoon of prayer warriors, but it takes the entire body coming together, gaining the vision, and knowing their gifts and their part in order for the war to be waged successfully. When we function together, working as a team in unity, we can and will be victorious!

1. Is your idea of the Christian walk that Jesus did all the work, so there is nothing you need to do?

2. Do you accept the fact that you are a soldier?

3. Do you know where you fit within the body God has placed you in?

4. Have you utilized the gifts God has given you by His Spirit?

5. Do you recognize the importance of unity within the body, members working together, using their gifts to further the Kingdom of God?

SOLDIERS

PART TWO

GOOD SOLDIERS

What will you do when no one else is looking?

A good soldier is not only good when they are being watched; they are good at all times. This doesn't mean we as believers don't mess up. It means our hearts and motives are right, and when we fall, we get back up, repent, and get back on the right path.

2 Timothy 2:3 and 4, "Endure thou therefore hardship as a good soldier of Jesus Christ. No man who warreth entangleth himself with the affairs of this life, that he may please him who hath chosen him to be a soldier."

You have been chosen by God to be a soldier. As a soldier who is in a war, there are some things that you must do in order to be that "good soldier."

YOU MUST CUT OFF THE ENEMY'S SUPPLY LINES.

What does that mean? During times of war, it is important for the enemy to have the supplies they need. They will need things like food, water, weapons, shelter. The supply lines are those places that the enemy can get in, the way they access what they need. It is an established line of travel or access.

You may be wondering, what are the established spiritual lines of travel or access that the enemies of your soul can get their supplies—the things they need to survive? Sin. Plain and simple, so how do you cut off the enemy's supply lines? Stay out of sin. Why?

Sin separates us from God. God will not dwell where sin is. Where God dwells there is power. We are cut off from the power of God working in our lives when we allow sin to dwell in us.

Deuteronomy 23:9, 14, "When the host goeth forth against thine enemies, then keep thyself from every evil thing… For the Lord thy God walketh in the midst of thy camp to deliver thee and to give up thine enemies before thee; therefore shall thy camp be holy, that He see no unclean thing in thee and turn away from you."

Wow! That's a humbling scripture when you dwell on it and its meaning.

How do we do this? How do we keep sin out of our lives?

Psalm 119:11, "Thy word have I hid in mine heart, that I might not sin against Thee."

When we hide God's word in our heart by studying it and meditating upon it, we can keep sin out.

Does this mean we will never sin? No, of course not, we are in a process of learning to get our flesh under the control of our spirit. Our flesh can be fed, and our spirit can be fed. If we feed our flesh and starve our spirit, our flesh will rule over us.

What do I mean by feeding our flesh? How do we do that?

I'm not speaking of eating and nourishing our bodies. That is necessary in order to take care of the temple of God. That is what our body is after all, and we should take care of it and nourish it, but think about it like this: if all you ever fed your physical body was junk food and sweets, would your physical body be healthy? No, it certainly would not. But if we eat healthy, an occasional sweet doesn't hurt us at all. Everything we do must be done in moderation.

Eating junk food and sweets all the time is, in fact, feeding the flesh because we are feeding desire. Entertainment can feed the flesh as well. There are many things that affect our flesh—our desires, and in moderation, they do not harm us, but if all we are doing is feeding that part of us and not feeding our spirit, the flesh takes control.

How do we feed the spirit? Praise, worship, prayer, meditation in God's Word, and fellowship with our brothers and sisters in Christ, these things feed our spirit and build us up, strengthening us.

What must we do when we realize we have sinned? Repent.

1 John 1:8 and 9, "If we say that we have no sin, we deceive ourselves and the truth is not in us. If we confess our sins, He is faithful and just to forgive us our sins, and to cleanse us from all unrighteousness."

1 John 2:1-2, "My little children, these things write I unto you, that ye sin not. And if any man sin, we have an advocate with the Father, Jesus Christ the righteous. And He is the propitiation for our sin, and not for ours only, but also for the sins of the whole world."

We all fall; we all sin, but we must confess our sins, repenting of them. Jesus is our advocate and our propitiation, our atoning victim.

What are the consequences of not repenting and continuing to walk in a particular sin?

We give access to Satan. If we do not repent, and we continue to walk in sin, we give Satan a place to operate in our lives. We cannot stand against Satan if we are in sin, and he cannot stand against us if we are walking in holiness. Let me be clear about what I mean by holiness. By holiness I mean that we walk in a state of repentance; therefore, His holiness is imputed to us. Remember Deuteronomy 23? When we keep ourselves from every evil thing, the

Lord walks in the midst of us and delivers us and gives up our enemies from before us.

Everything that Satan brings against you in your life is to try and get you to walk in sin so that he will have that access. He has to have a supply line in order to live. Cut off the supply line by walking in daily repentance.

Are you a soldier? Are you a good soldier? Do you want to be a good soldier? Have you cut off the enemy's supply lines?

YOU MUST STAY IN CONTACT WITH YOUR SUPERIOR.

Who is your superior? First and foremost, Jesus Christ is your superior. He is the head.

Colossians 1:18, "And He (Jesus) is the head of the body, the church. He is the beginning, the first-born from the dead, that in all things He might have the preeminence."

Secondly, those in leadership within your church body have been placed there by God for a purpose.

Ephesians 4:11-13, "And He appointed some to be apostles, and some prophets, and some evangelists, and some pastors, and teachers, for the perfecting of the saints for the work of the ministry, and for the edifying of the body of Christ, until we all come into the unity of the faith and of the knowledge of the Son of God, and become perfect men, unto the measure of the stature of the fullness of Christ."

Now, let me make this clear right up front, by superior, I am not suggesting that those in leadership within the body of Christ are "superior" to you as defined—higher in quality, better than others, or condescending. What I'm referring to here is higher in rank, position, or authority. Yes, there is authority within the church. It is not a dictatorship and should not be, but those in authority are held to a higher standard.

2 Corinthians 10:8, "For though I should boast somewhat more of our authority, which the Lord hath given us for edification, and not for your destruction, I should not be ashamed."

Authority is given to those called into leadership for edification, not destruction.

Hebrews 13:7, "Remember those who have the rule over you, who have spoken unto you the Word of God. Follow their faith, considering the outcome of their manner of living."

Hebrews 13:17, "Obey those who have the rule over you and submit yourselves, for they keep watch over your souls as ones who must give an account, that they may do it with joy and not with grief, for that is unprofitable for you."

The word rule in both situations comes from a Greek word that means to lead, those in official command, not by dictating but rather by leading. Those God has placed you under for edification will have to give an account, not only for their choices and decisions, but for the way they led those placed under them.

I Corinthians 11:1, "Be ye followers of me, even as I also am of Christ."

Why is it important to stay in contact with your superior?

A soldier has to stay in communication with his superiors so that he can receive instructions and or counsel. God has given us our leaders within the body for our edification. If we are not communicating with them, we are not receiving the edification the Lord desires for us to have. If we are not attending church regularly, we are missing out on this communication.

Proverbs 24:6, "For by wise counsel thou shalt wage thy war, and in the multitude of counselors there is safety."

What kind of instructions will you be receiving? If you stay in contact with your superior, your superior will inform you of the whereabouts of the enemy. He will let you know what is going on around you. He will show you the direction you should be heading and inform you of the direction you are presently going, revealing if it is right or wrong. He will guide you in what you are supposed to be doing at any given moment, and he will reveal what is expected of you at the time.

If we receive instructions by staying in communication with our superior, how do we go about communicating with God and those placed in authority within the church?

Through prayer we communicate with Jesus. Would you enjoy a conversation that was one sided? No, I think not. People that never allow others to get a word in edge wise are annoying. Likewise, we cannot have one sided conversations with God. He desires to communicate with us as well.

How does He do that? He talks to us through the still, small voice, His Word, a pricking in the heart, words of wisdom and prophecy, and signs. The Holy Spirit will shed light into the darkness surrounding us and expose the enemy encroaching upon us. He will make visible the traps the enemy has laid out before us. He will reveal the tactics the enemy plans to use in order to capture, wound, or ensnare us.

Through staying in contact with the leadership within the body, we are made aware of the enemies' attacks upon the body. This gives us the ability to stand unified against the enemy so that we can organize and strategize to press forward into the darkness and against the darkness. We find out who amongst us has been afflicted, wounded, beaten down, and trapped. Then as a unified army (because the army of the Living God does not leave a soldier behind), we are able to find that brother or sister, gather around them, help to heal their wounds, guard them from further attacks, and fight on their behalf!

As we come together (holding up our shields of faith in front of us all), the line behind us holds up their shields above us all—creating a covering, a protective barrier. In order to pull this off, the church must be closely knit together. Separation within this grouping leaves a hole, a place the enemy can get in. That is why we need the whole body to stay in unity. Jesus prayed that very thing. He prayed for the church that we would be one, even as He and the Father were one. Why? So that the world would believe that the Father had sent Him. Think about that for a minute…Unity within the body is not just important; it is crucial.

Look at the critics around us in this world right now. Many do not believe that Jesus is who He says He is simply because of the bickering and backbiting they see within the church. Division is one of the enemy's biggest tactics. If we allow Satan to divide us, we cannot press forward into the darkness and push back the gates of Hell. Think about it like this. We are called to go into gross darkness and shine our light. Each of us has the Light of God within us, but one single candle can only bring so much light to a darkened room. Imagine the darkness we can expel when we go forward together, in unity, combining the light each of us have.

A good soldier knows the tactics of the enemy they are fighting. **(2 Corinthians 2:11)**

(I Peter 5:8) He is out there seeking whom he may devour. He uses his clever devices to accomplish this. Don't be deceived; Satan is clever; he is sly; he knows the Word of God, and he knows your weaknesses. So, what are those tactics he uses? His tactics are division in the body, oppression, deceptions, lies, twisting the Word of God, separating a soldier from his troop, and the temptation to sin—giving him a supply line.

How does he implement his tactics? **(Revelation 12:15)** He opened his mouth and spewed out water. What comes out of your mouth? Words. He carries out his plans to defeat the church by speaking lies and deceptions in our minds, twisting the Word of God. He uses words to turn us against one another and to tempt us to sin. Know your enemy. Learn to recognize his voice, and take his words captive, dispelling them.

1. Are you a good soldier?

2. Have you cut off the enemies' supply lines in your life, eliminating sin?

3. Have you stayed in contact with your superiors, Jesus as the commander and the leadership within the church God has placed you in?

4. Have you isolated yourself, cutting off that communication and making yourself vulnerable to attacks by the enemy?

5. Do you recognize the enemy's voice when he speaks?

IN CHRIST

I Peter 5:14, "…Peace be with you all who are **in Christ** Jesus. Amen."

Are you in Christ? That is an important question that needs a serious answer. In order to properly answer that question, let us first ask ourselves another question.

What does it mean to be in Christ?

Imagine a baby that is growing inside his mother's womb. That baby is totally dependent upon the mother for nutrition and safety. That baby's world is completely surrounded by the mother. She encompasses the baby. When people look at her, they don't see the baby, they see her. Others can see evidence that she is carrying a baby, but they cannot see the baby.

To be in Christ is to be totally dependent upon Him for everything, to be encompassed by Him. We should be so surrounded by Jesus that when others look at us they see Him. Yes, there will be evidence of it being us. We will sound the same and look the same, but we will be different.

What does the Word tell us about being in Christ?

We hear about the grace of God all the time. We've been told and we've read in the Word that we are saved by that grace. How did we receive that grace? We received God's grace by faith, by believing, but where is that grace?

2 Timothy 2:1, "Thou therefore, my son, be strong in the grace that is **in** Christ Jesus."

In order to receive God's grace, which is in Christ, we must be in Christ as well. Faith, belief, is a transporter that translates us from the natural into the supernatural. It takes us from our natural surroundings and places us within the spiritual realm into Jesus Himself.

Imagine you're sitting by an in-ground pool soaking up the sun. You're leaning back, lounging. You're outside of the pool. How do you go about getting into the pool? You have to move from where you are and get up off that lounge chair and get into the pool.

The same is true of being in Christ. Before Christ comes into your life, before you hear the Word of God that tells you Jesus died for your sins, you are going through life outside of Him. Inside your spirit there is a seed that needs watering. It is faith. God gave every human a portion of faith, but it is inactive like a dormant seed.

Romans 12:3, "…God hath dealt to every man the measure of faith."

Faith is there within your spirit, but it is lying dormant until it germinates. How does it germinate?

Romans 10:17, "So then faith cometh by hearing, and hearing by the Word of God."

Faith will spring forth from that seed when it is watered by God's Word. Before you could come to Christ, you had to hear that He was seeking you out to save you, but first, you had to hear some bad news. You had to be told you were lost. You already knew it deep down inside, but you had to come to the realization that the emptiness you felt, the hole in your heart, the longing for understanding why you came into this world, all of these things existed within you because you were lost in a dark world.

Once you came to the place of realizing you needed a savior, you had to hear the good news (the gospel) that Jesus had come to redeem us. He stepped down from the glory of heaven and came into the darkness shining His light to show us the way and to take the sin of the world upon Himself so that we all could be washed clean through His blood.

Faith is that activator that translates us. It moves us from being outside that pool and immerses us into it.

Romans 6:3, "Know ye not that as many of us as were baptized into Jesus Christ were baptized into His death?"

Faith immerses us into Jesus, baptizing us into Him His death, so what does that mean exactly?

2 Corinthians 5:17, "Therefore if any man be **in** Christ, he is a new creature: old things are passed away; behold, all things have become new."

By being baptized into the death of Jesus, we are made new creatures. We are no longer the same.

What are some of the ways of a new creature?

Romans 8:1 and 2, "There is therefore now no condemnation for those who are in Christ Jesus, who walk not according to the flesh, but according to the Spirit. For the law of the Spirit of life in Christ Jesus hath made me free from the law of sin and death."

When we are in Christ, the guilt of our sin from our past life is gone. We may still feel guilty for things we have done, but we are no longer held accountable for them by God. We are no longer condemned for them, but this is only if we walk not according to the flesh.

When we are in Christ, we are free from the law of sin and death.

I Corinthians 4:17, "For this cause I have sent unto you Timothy, who is my beloved son and faithful in the Lord, who shall put you in remembrance of my ways which are in Christ."

The Apostle Paul tells us that his ways are in Christ, and we are to be reminded of the way he walked because our ways should be in Christ as well.

To be in Christ is to no longer be seen. When God looks at you, He sees Jesus. When others look at you, they should see Jesus as well because we are hidden in Him. We are His representation in this world. We should go about doing good just as He did. We should be healing the sick, raising the dead, and cleansing the leper.

We are in Him, and the Kingdom of God is within us! The enemy can no longer get to us unless we give him access. The law of sin and death no longer has power over us. We are no longer captive to do the will of sin or the devil. We are free. We are free from our old lives. We are free to live a holy life, and we have access to God's power to bring that same freedom to the lost world.

1. Are your ways in Christ?

2. Are you in Christ?

3. Are you completely dependent upon God?

4. When people see you, do they see Christ?

5. Have you tapped into the faith required to translate you into Christ?

6. Are you a new creature? Have your old ways passed away?

7. Are you walking according to the Spirit or according to the flesh?

8. Are you free? Are you taking that same freedom to the lost world?

9. Are you becoming an armed soldier in Christ?

OBJECT LESSONS AND GAMES

Here is a list of object lessons and games that can be used when teaching the lessons.

BECOMING PART ONE:

Caterpillar/Butterfly

The first section of Becoming focuses on what you are becoming. You are becoming the image of Christ. To show something in nature as to how this takes place, we can look at the life cycle of the caterpillar into a butterfly.

Butterflies go through four cycles in life.

The first cycle is the egg. Let's imagine that the egg is like the soul of a human housing the spirit, which has yet to receive the life of Christ.

The second stage of the cycle is the larva, the caterpillar. This is similar to the human body the soul and spirit are placed within. The caterpillar eats and grows until it is time to change.

The third stage is the Chrysalis. This is considered to be one of the coolest stages in the natural, and the same is true of the spiritual picture we are examining. This represents a time of rest amidst rapid change. A hard, outer shell forms around the caterpillar. Imagine this is grave clothes that are wrapped around us that have been soaked in the blood of Jesus. This is the point that we conceive the life of God. We die to ourselves and begin to change as we are being formed into the image of Christ. The caterpillar is resting yet changing, just as we rest from our works and enter into a time of allowing Jesus to make the changes within us.

Inside the cocoon a metamorphosis is taking place. Inside of a child of God a transformation is taking place as well.

The fourth stage is when the butterfly emerges from the cocoon as a new, beautiful creature. The end result of the transformations Jesus makes within us during that time of our life is: we are a new creature. We are in the image of God.

Pictures of the butterfly stages can be found online and printed to use while going over the object lesson.

BECOMING PART TWO:

Cleansing the mind

Needed items: Empty, clear water bottles, food coloring, and bleach.

Fill one bottle with pure bleach. This bottle represents the Word of God. You can label it. Fill the other bottle halfway with water. Put several drops of food coloring in it, enough to make it look dark. This bottle represents the mind of the believer. When we first come to God our minds are full of darkness.

As you are sharing about how the Word of God cleanses the mind, pour small amounts of bleach (the Word) into the bottle. The bleach will lighten the colored water little by little showing how cleansing your mind is a process that takes place slowly as we fill our minds with the Word of God.

ARMED PART ONE:

Possessing the Land

Items needed: Checker board and pieces.

Use the checker board to represent the world. The red checkers are symbolic of the believers who have been covered by the blood of Jesus, and the side they are set upon when the game starts represents the territory in this world we as believers have conquered and must protect from invasion. The black checkers represent the powers of darkness, and their side of the board is the lost world they control. Checkers is a strategic game—thought must be given before moving a piece. The idea is to invade the other side's territory and take out as many of their checker pieces as possible. Do not be deceived; that is the enemy's sole purpose as well, to take out as many believers as he can in order to keep them from invading the territory he rules.

ARMED PART TWO:

The Armor

Needed items: Roman armor. You can purchase this online in costume section of Amazon.

As you go through teaching about each piece of the armor, you can have someone serve as a model, putting each piece on and giving a visual for the teaching.

SOLDIERS PART ONE:

Unified

Needed items: Rope or old shoelaces. Need at least four volunteers to demonstrate teamwork. This can be done when you get to the section titled Teamwork.

Use the shoelaces or rope to tie the teams' legs together, like in a three-legged race, but do not stop at two people. Tie the second person's leg to the third person's leg, and so forth and so on. The only leg not tied to another should be the two people on the end of the line. Give them a finish line. They will need to discuss who uses which leg first as they walk in unity to the finish line.

We are all joined together by the Holy Spirit, and we are all headed together toward the same goal.

Ask one in the middle to attempt going in a different direction than the rest and see the result. Ask one of them in the middle to simply stop moving forward.

Point out how it is necessary to work together, in unity, to make it to their goal. It takes each of us doing our part.

SOLDIERS PART TWO:
Contact

Items needed: blindfold and obstacles set up. It can be as simple as chairs set in path, rope, or an old tire, anything to create an obstacle course.

Choose one person from the group to be the believer needing guidance through the obstacle course of life. Before session pick someone to represent Jesus and someone to represent the devil. The believer you picked is not to know who they should follow. Each person should be speaking out instructions on how to make it through the obstacle course. The person representing the devil should be trying to deceive the person, causing them to run into the obstacles.

This lesson is used to teach us how important it is to know the voice of God and to learn to recognize the voice of the enemy. When we hear a voice that guides us in one direction, and when that particular direction leads us into a trap or a snare, we need to learn to recognize that voice so that we know when the enemy is attempting to lead us astray.

IN CHRIST:

Needed items: a dried sponge and a bowl of water.

The bowl of water represents Christ. The dried sponge represents the old man, the you before giving your life to Jesus. Talk about how the dryness of the sponge is the old ways that need to change. Place the sponge in the bowl of water and watch as the sponge becomes new. Being in Christ makes the old man pass away and causes a new man to arise. Point out that if you take the sponge out of the water, out of Christ, the sponge will eventually dry out and the old ways will resurface.